8

Things
Every Boy
Should Know
About Being
a Man

8

Things Every Boy Should Know About Being a Man

BY HORACE HOUGH

First Edition: May 2019

Book design by Baily Crawford

ISBN-13: 978-1-7330195-0-7 (paperback)

ISBN-13: 978-1-7330195-1-4 (ebook)

Published by Bethune and Nest, LLC

167 Cherry Street, Suite# 309

Milford, CT 06460

www.horacehoughauthor.com

TO SHAKII—TOLD YOU I WOULD WRITE IT.

An old man going a lone highway,
Came at the evening, cold and gray,
To a chasm, vast, and deep and wide,
Through which was flowing a sullen tide.

The old man crossed in the twilight dim;
The sullen stream had no fear for him;
But he turned, when safe on the other side,
And built a bridge to span the tide.

"Old man," said a fellow pilgrim, near,
"You are wasting strength with building here;
Your journey will end with the ending day;
You never again will pass this way;
You've crossed the chasm, deep and wide—
Why build you this bridge at the evening tide?"

The builder lifted his old gray head:
"Good friend, in the path I have come," he said,
"There followeth after me today,
A youth, whose feet must pass this way.

This chasm, that has been naught to me,
To that fair-haired youth may a pitfall be.
He, too, must cross in the twilight dim;
Good friend, I am building this bridge for him."

-"*THE BRIDGE BUILDER,*" WILL ALLEN DROMGOOLE

CONTENTS

INTRODUCTION

AFTER WORKING WITH urban youth for over fifteen years, there are two serious things I've noticed about boys. The first is obvious—many boys struggle with learning how to become men. Moreover, many of these same boys do not have men in their lives as positive examples. The second is that these same boys live in a society that absolutely needs and expects them to grow into men. Sadly, they cannot do this without direction. Mixing their struggle and lack of direction with society's expectation creates a dangerous problem.

When boys begin to reach their teenage years, everywhere they turn, someone is looking for them to do something that seems impossible; someone is challenging them to use an inordinate amount of self-control; someone is causing them pain and sadness but expecting them to use superior self-restraint and act like nothing is bothering them; someone is expecting to be protected by their strength, lifted by their support, and comforted by their understanding. And it seems as if *everyone* is waiting to ridicule them and call them less than men if they do not live up to these expectations.

The life of a man who does not live up to these expectations is one full of confusion, pain, desperation, lack of identity, searching, rejection, and mistakes. This leads to hurting those he loves, not building family and community, picking up destructive habits, and avoiding responsibility. Judgment and derision by the world—other men, women, and maybe even himself—is the only likely outcome.

There are many men in our society who have never learned some of the basic things that every boy should know about being a man. There are also men who have learned these things but have chosen not to live their lives accordingly. They significantly add to this problem of boys not being prepared for manhood, because boys who are looking for an example are following in these men's flawed footsteps.

Over the years, I have found that I keep attempting to teach the same lessons over and over again to boys who do not have positive male examples. At times, even boys who are lucky to have a good man in their lives need to hear these lessons as well. This book contains some of those lessons.

Some of the following points may apply to a boy right now, some may apply as he gets older, and some may even apply to men. These may just be needed reminders. Nevertheless, I hope that this book will help any boy or man who may need guidance or encouragement.

8 Things Every Boy Should Know about Being a Man is my attempt to help young men along the winding and difficult road that is manhood. There are many more than eight things to learn, but learning eighty things without these eight would not be helpful. I believe that these few lessons will form a solid foundation for boys who are trying to grow into men. I am not an expert on manhood, nor do I think that I have all the answers. I am still striving to be a better man myself. I have been lucky to have men take time to build a bridge for me to cross; I hope to do the same for others. As men, we're in this journey together. And it starts with an open conversation.

ONE

IT IS HARD

HE WAS TIRED OF the yelling, but it would not stop. He learned a long time ago that it was better to take the screaming rather than try to stop it. Last time he tried, well, it didn't go well.

"I can't believe you would say something like that to an adult!" his mother shouted.

"I don't know who you think you are!" his dad immediately followed. "We raised you to be better than that!" His father stormed out, mumbling to himself, "I can't even stand looking at you." The door slammed with so much force that the entire house shook.

His mother was quietly staring at him with a look of rage. When she lifted her hand, he thought she was going to slap him again. Instead, she reached across the table to grab another cigarette. Lighting it, she said, "I don't care what that other boy did to you . . ." She blew smoke out of her nose as she thought about what she was trying to say. "You just can't do that."

Out of the corner of his eye, he saw his uncle gazing at him while sitting in a chair on the other side of the kitchen. He didn't want to look in his uncle's direction; he knew that he disappointed him.

"Go to your room until I figure out what to do with you," his mother sneered through thick smoke.

The boy stood up quickly, knocking over the chair, and stormed off toward the bedroom.

"I can't stand this house," he yelled before slamming his bedroom door closed. But it didn't close.

His uncle caught the door and ran into the room so fast

that the boy did not have time to react. The boy stumbled and fell backward against the wall. His uncle had him pinned. The man towered over his nephew and stood so close that the boy could feel the breath coming out of his nostrils. The man was furious. In his entire young life, the boy had never seen him like this.

"Don't you dare blow up like that again," he whispered. It was not only a command; it was a threat.

The boy was more upset than scared now. He screamed, "So I'm just supposed to sit there while I get treated like crap?"

"In this situation? Yes."

"That's stupid! That doesn't make sense! You didn't hear what the other boy said about Mom! And then the teacher said if I had better parents . . ." He heard his voice crack. It felt like he had a golf ball in his throat.

"Look," his uncle said softly, "I know that life has to be hard right now. Your dad and your mom haven't figured out if they're going to try and make their marriage work. Your mom is

3

not working, so you had to give up track and work more shifts. I get that. I know that your dad's drinking has you worried. It worries me too. And I know that you are having a rough time with your classmates. And I don't even know what your relationship is like with your girlfriend. I'm sorry. If I were in your position at your age, I would have broken by now. But you're stronger than that."

"No, I'm not," the boy said while trying to hold back tears.

The uncle looked at his nephew's watery eyes and reddened face. "Yes, you are," he said. "You just don't believe it yet because you're hurting, and like most men, that kind of hurt makes you mad. But you have to keep your head on straight. No more blowing up.

"Listen, I'm going to tell you what you may never hear from another man again. Being a man is hard."

You may never hear this on the radio. You may never see it on a talk show. Your favorite music artist may never perform a song about it. Honestly, you may never hear this from another man as long as you live.

Being a man is hard.

That does not mean women do not struggle as well, or that their lives are not filled with burdens we cannot begin to imagine (many of them caused by men). But being a man has a specific set of challenges.

Everyone has his and her own personal struggles. Along with those personal struggles, we also have challenges we face as part of our different communities and social groups. For example, there are unique struggles if you are Black, Hispanic, Asian, Caucasian, gay or lesbian, Muslim, Jewish, or an immigrant or first generation; if English is not your first language; if you are poor, rich, or middle class; if you live in the city, country, or suburbs; if you are young or old; and especially if you are a woman or a man.

We, as adult men, spend a lot of time trying to get

through our struggles and expect other men to quietly do the same. Most of the time, we never stop to prepare young men to face the fact that being a man in this culture takes work. So many boys and men end up looking to drugs or destructive behavior, or they simply give up and commit suicide because they were not ready for the challenges of manhood. People expect you to automatically be a man. No one thinks about how difficult it may be for some boys and men to live up to that expectation. It's not hard because boys are weak or soft. It's hard because it is just that—hard.

Every morning when a man wakes up, as he swings his legs out of bed, he has to decide, "I am going to be a 'man' today. No matter what happens, no matter how much I hurt, no matter how many times I mess up, no matter how much I want to do something reckless, irresponsible, or selfish, I'm going to be a 'man' today." The decision is not always made consciously or said out loud. However, every day every man has to make that choice.

Men don't automatically learn this as they get older.

There are many of us who never learned what it takes to successfully become a man. So eventually, many men become angry and rebellious when the world starts looking for them to live up to its challenging expectations. Many boys and men never imagined that it would be so hard. All of a sudden, people start expecting you to do things that are so difficult, you feel that it's not realistic or possible. If you never thought that being a man was hard, then the challenges of manhood, the responsibilities that you are supposed to take care of, and the fact that people expect so much from you will feel like the world is picking on you for not being Superman.

Some men learn this lesson because situations in their lives force them to make the adjustment and step up to the challenge. Yet most men learn that it is hard from watching other men. In the same way many toddler boys mimic their fathers or male examples, boys also learn how hard it is to be a man from watching other men struggle and win, or struggle and lose. Seeing how other men react to difficult moments is how boys learn to deal with struggle and handle hard times. Learning this way can be good or bad, depending on the example set by the other man. But what if there is no real example? What if the example is a bad one? Now, the young man is left to figure everything out on his own.

So, just in case you didn't have an example or your example was not a good one; just in case you've been following the examples of celebrity athletes, music artists, reality television stars, or actors; just in case you've been trying to follow advice such as "man up," "get over it," and "suck it up"; in case you have followed all that advice and all those examples, and none of it is making anything easier, remember this: being a man is hard. If all men knew the difficulty and accepted it, then we would all be much more prepared for the challenges ahead. The more prepared they are, the less boys and men will give up or become self-destructive. Always know that you are going through what other men have gone through. You are facing what other men have met and conquered.

From me to you, man to man, it *is* hard. Yet, like so many men who have lived successful and happy lives before you, it is doable, it is manageable, and it is winnable.

MANHOOD CHALLENGE: Every morning,
wake up and expect to work hard. Make the choice to handle all your difficult moments in the best way possible.

Two

You're Not as Mad as You Think You Are

THE GRADE ON HIS paper confirmed it: he had failed another test. His parents were going to be upset, and his older brothers would make fun of him by calling him stupid. It had been that way his entire life.

Maybe I don't have to let my parents know. As if she could read his mind, he heard his teacher announce, "Make sure you take your paper home, get it signed, and bring it back tomorrow."

His hand immediately flew into the air to get her attention. "What happens if we don't get it signed?"

"Just get it signed."

"But I don't know when my mom—"

"Just get it signed," his teacher repeated wearily. "You ask the same questions after every test—always trying to find a way to get out of having your test signed."

Was he embarrassed? Yes. Was he upset that she spoke to him that way? Yes. Was he more worried about telling his parents that he failed another test? Yes.

He really had studied. At least, he thought he had. He tried as hard as possible, but looking at information for hours never worked for him. He once had a tutor who taught him a trick to better remember what he was studying. He improved on quizzes for a while, but the tutor eventually moved away to another state. Without any help, his grades dropped again, and his brothers went back to laughing and calling him stupid.

Honestly, he felt that his parents thought he was stupid as well.

While leaning over to put the paper in his book bag, he saw some of his football teammates on the other side of the classroom laughing at him for failing yet another test. They were normally good friends, but they always made fun of everyone, including themselves, if they thought something was funny.

He left the classroom in a rush as soon as the bell rang.

"Watch out," a girl sneered at him. "You're just going to bump into me and not say 'excuse me'?"

Distracted, he bumped a few more people as he walked through the crowded hallway. He was thinking about the test so much, he never realized that his heart was beating rapidly and that his breathing was becoming heavy. He had to try seven times to open his locker; his hands were shaking.

He turned to go to his next class when he saw his teammates and friends who were with him from the previous period.

"You'll be all right," said his best friend while patting

him on the back. "Your mom knows that you're stupid."

He actually felt his friend's nose break behind the force of his fist. He punched him so hard that he knocked him out in one hit. He was in a rage. He saw one of the other kids who laughed at him in the classroom, grabbed him by the shirt, and shoved him into the lockers. He threw another heavy punch, but the boy ducked and tackled him.

He was pinned on the floor. It didn't matter how upset he was now. He was on the bottom of a fight that he was about to lose. He took one punch to the face. Two punches. Three. He wasn't strong enough to get up. He tried to protect himself, but he was not fast enough to block the swings. All he could do was cover up and take the beating.

In the school office, he sat with ice on his face, waiting to get picked up by his dad. His father had to leave a business meeting at the studio to come and get him. It would normally be his mother picking him up, but she was on a flight back home from a business trip to Hong Kong.

The other boy in the fight, the one who everyone said won, got suspended for three days and had already been picked up by his mother. However, he wasn't going to be so lucky. He was suspended until the principal and staff could have a meeting with both of his parents.

He rearranged the ice so that a colder spot could touch his eye. Leaning his head back against the wall and adjusting in the uncomfortable office chair, he saw his coach walk in. The coach sat down next to him but stayed quiet. The boy didn't know what to say. But he knew what he felt. Shame.

After some time, his coach whispered, "Considering that my all-state quarterback is now out with a broken nose and both my star running back and linebacker are out with suspensions for fighting, I am the best person to have this conversation." He looked at the boy in his one un-iced eye. "As a man, there is something that you should know. Sometimes when you're sad, it looks like anger. Sometimes you're confused, but it looks like anger. Sometimes you're even afraid, and it looks like anger."

He pulled out a piece of gum and offered it to the boy.

The boy's head hurt just thinking about chewing. "No, thank you," the boy said.

The coach shrugged his shoulders, put the gum in his mouth, and continued. "You're not as mad as you think you are. Learn to be honest with yourself and deal with the feelings that you have. Stop taking anger out on everyone. It will keep you out of a lot of bad situations. Sometimes you are just sad and confused. Sometimes you are embarrassed. Sometimes you are just hurt."

His coach took a deep breath and stood up. "Now I'm going to go and try to win this championship game without my star players." He began to walk out of the office, then stopped. Without turning around, he said, "And no, I'm not mad. I'm disappointed."

Men generally show two emotions: happiness and anger. However, anger is the one that most people remember seeing us express. Why? Because when men show their anger, it is usually aggressive, possibly violent, and on many occasions, sudden and extreme—in other words, very memorable. Along with that, there are even some men who seem to be angry all the time. Why are we so angry? Why are we so mad?

Every boy, every young man, and even some adult men need to know that they are not as mad as they think they are. We feel the same variety of emotions as everyone else. What is different with us is how we express those emotions and show our feelings. By the time many boys make it to puberty or adolescence, they have already become experts at showing only those two feelings of happiness and anger.

Think about this: a sad man looks like a mad man, a hurt man looks like a mad man, and even a confused or vulnerable man looks like a mad man. Everyone has seen a man who is physically hurt react with anger. If he stubs his toe on a chair, he may hit the chair; if he hits his head on a cabinet door, he may hit the cabinet; even if he is sad, he may get upset and yell at people who ask him if something is wrong. It seems that every unpleasant emotion men have looks like anger. Many boys get into fights and arguments and make bad life choices because they only know how to express one feeling. And when taken to the extreme, this can also hurt others. Many school shootings, mass killings, and violent acts are committed by young men who feel overwhelmed with different emotions and display them as one: anger.

We are not always as upset or angry as we think we are. We just don't know many other ways to express our feelings. That frustration of not having other ways to show our emotions begins to look like anger. Now we start looking like the stereotypical angry man. Honestly, many people would be uncomfortable if we started showing other emotions, because anger is what is expected of us. Feeling angry so often is not healthy physically, mentally, or emotionally. It can become a burden that is too much to handle. What's even worse is that men begin to really believe that they don't experience other uncomfortable emotions such as pain, sadness, and fear. "I'm OK," "I'm not scared," and "I'm not hurt" become common ways to deal with these emotions that we don't understand.

From a very early age, boys are trained to cover up and not act on their emotions. Young boys are taught not to cry, to "toughen up," to "walk it off," and to "suck it up." We are also trained not to show any level of frustration or anger toward people who are in authority. We learn not to talk out of turn, to avoid making facial expressions to show our annoyances, and to never show fear of anything. To do these things would have us labeled "not a man" or "less than a man."

But that is not where it ends.

Boys are constantly and intentionally challenged to see if they will slip up and respond in ways they shouldn't ... especially by other boys and men. Every teenage boy has had someone act like they are going to hit him, and if you flinch (which looks like you are afraid), you lose a few manhood points. Someone will intentionally and constantly chastise a boy, getting in his face, pushing him to the limit of his self-control, and insulting him if he shows the smallest amount of frustration. The idea is to force boys to turn into what some people think a man is. Or shame them for not being tough enough. It can be very hard to deal with if you are not used to it. More than that, it makes it difficult to know the emotions you are feeling and even harder to express them.

Our society and culture do not leave a lot of room for men who openly express the entire range of their feelings. There are some people who will try to make you feel comfortable showing your emotions; sadly, many of those same exact people will surprisingly and quickly become annoyed or judgmental of this new emotional you. Although their minds will know that you should not be judged as "less than a man" or, even worse, as "acting like a girl" (which is insulting to women), many men, as well as women, do not expect that kind of behavior from men.

Added to this, you may think that talking to guys about your feelings would help. You may think, *They understand what I'm going through, right?* Almost every boy alive learns very quickly and very easily that trying to talk to another guy about your emotions is close to useless. Well, *useless* may be the wrong word. *Complicated* is a better term. Men don't manage their own

feelings well, so trying to deal with *someone else's* feelings is . . .
again, complicated. There are three general responses that you
will get from a man who wants to be helpful and talk to you
about emotions. There are different versions and sometimes
different answers, but most of them work like this:

1. If he wants to be helpful, he will give you some
    logical advice that will make you think about the sit-
    uation but will not help you with how you feel.

2. He may encourage you not to act on your feelings
    and just do what it takes to be a man.

3. He may just tell you to "man up" and "stop act-
    ing like a (fill in the blank with whatever you have
    heard)."

Now, it's not useless advice. There are things you
absolutely need to know in that list of responses. Furthermore,
and for the record, men have a very valuable and effective way

of communicating that works well for us. That will be addressed in the next chapter. However, the mentioned answers will only help you with showing (or not showing) your emotions. They will not help you deal with feeling them but still not being able to express them. What is frighteningly worse is that men who cannot acknowledge and deal with their emotions may turn to drugs, alcohol, mistreating women, violence, and even suicide as a way to handle their pain.

So where does that leave us? Listen, I don't have all the answers. After all, I am a man who also deals with these same issues. Yet, I can offer you this:

1. DON'T BE FOOLED BY THE STEREOTYPE

Someone lied and said that men are not emotional. That is a dangerous stereotype. It is true that we are taught *not to show* our feelings, but that doesn't mean that we don't have them. Men have the same emotions as women. Be true to yourself, and be honest about what you are feeling. You may not always be able to act on your emotions, but know that they are there. You will tell people that you are "OK," "fine," and "all right" when things may really bother you. We all do it. We don't want to talk about it. We don't want anyone talking to us about it. We just want to be left alone and get back to whatever we were doing before we were bothered in the first place. But don't believe your own lies. Pay attention to whether you are sad, hurt, lonely, etc. If you know what you feel, you can find a way to address it. You can work on being happy if you know you're sad. You can work on being healed if you know you are hurting. You can work on taking care of how you feel, as long as you know what you are feeling. Again, don't be fooled by the stereotype.

2. FIND A *HEALTHY* WAY TO DEAL WITH YOUR FEELINGS

We already know that talking to random people may not work for everyone, but there is always a parent, family member, or friend you can speak with. If you do not have anyone, maybe you can find a counselor (for example, psychiatrist, minister, or advocate). You can also write in a journal. Some of you just frowned or laughed and decided that you are definitely not doing that. Still, it is a good idea and often very helpful for a lot of men. The point is to know what you feel and find a healthy way to deal with it that does not damage you or anyone else. Every man who is successful in life has to find his own way to handle this. You must also find yours.

3. STOP OVERLY EXPRESSING YOUR ANGER

Just because you feel angry doesn't mean that you have to *show* anger. Expressing yourself in an angry way will almost always make a situation worse than when it started. So stop expressing it. Even when you are actually upset, find a way to make the situation better. Find a way to fix it. Find a solution. Too many men express anger simply because that is what they feel, and they make the situation a thousand times worse. This can lead to aggression or senseless violence. Understand, we all make mistakes with showing anger. Still, we all should look for a better way to deal with our feelings.

When modern-day bridges were first being constructed, they were built with strong, unbendable materials. This was a problem. In certain areas, because of the wind, earthquakes, and other forces, the bridges would break. It was then that the suspension bridge was invented. This brilliant idea let the bridges swing, move, and bend so that they could remain standing unlike the immovable ones that would crumple. After they finish swaying and bending, they go back to their original shape.

Being overwhelmed is bending. Losing your confidence is bending. Showing sadness is bending. Crying is bending. But always know that bending doesn't make you weak. Many times, it helps you get through the metaphorical earthquakes and rough periods of your life without breaking. Just get yourself back together, and keep on standing strong.

Dealing with emotions is difficult. Honestly, you may not always get it right. However, if you become good at it, you will lead a life that will have many more positive opportunities. Be honest with yourself. Sometimes things are going to hurt, be confusing, make you feel uncomfortable, and maybe even make you weak—but don't let that make you feel like less than a man. Those are just bending moments, and everyone who is strong must bend.

Remember, you are not as mad (or emotionless) as you think you are. You know the feelings that you have when no one is looking. When the door to your room is closed and the light is off, you know how rough it can be. You are much more complex than being a person who only feels happy or angry. As hard as it may seem, be honest with yourself, and try to work through your emotions. You will be a stronger and better man for it.

MANHOOD CHALLENGE: Why are you upset?
Be honest with yourself about your emotions. Try to figure out what you are truly feeling.

Three

You Don't Want to Talk about It . . . Because You Can't

This was getting bad.

His mother would not stop asking questions.

"Sweetheart, talk to me," she said while holding his hand. "At least look at me."

They were sitting across from each other. Her knees were touching his. Her hands were holding his. She was sitting with her elbows on her thighs trying to understand what he was going through.

"Baby," she continued, "something is obviously wrong."

His heart was pounding so hard he could see it through his T-shirt. His face looked blank and free of emotion, but his eyes couldn't keep up the lie. He began to cry. No sobbing, no sniffing, no sound—just tears.

"Tell me what's wrong," she pleaded with fresh tears running down her own cheeks. She dropped her head. "Is there something that I'm missing? What are you not telling me?"

He wanted to get up and walk away, but he could not let go of her hands. He needed her there to feel better.

"Baby, I need to know why you have a gun."

It was lying on the table next to them. She found it while looking for some old family pictures that she used to keep in his room. The only reason that he left it at home was because he knew that school security would be checking everyone for weapons. Ever since gunshots rang out in the hallway two weeks ago, they had been doing very thorough searches.

Three nights ago, his mother had walked in on him while he was crying. He had just gotten off the phone when he stood up and suddenly punched through the wall. When she came to find out what the noise was, he was pacing in a circle with a bloody hand balled up into a fist.

Later that same night, she signed into Facebook and Twitter to look at his posts to see if something was going on. All she saw was a string of "LOL" comments left on his Facebook page.

"Baby, say something. What's going on? Say something. Do you need someone to talk to? A counselor or someone?"

"No," he said clearly.

"I can't just let this go. I'm worried, and you need to tell me something!"

He opened his mouth slowly as she waited for a response. "I . . . I just . . . I," he stammered. "I . . ." Then he closed his mouth and dropped his head. She couldn't see his face. All she saw were his tears dripping onto his shirt.

We, as boys and men, know that we don't want to talk about how we feel. What many of us don't know is that many times, we can't talk about it.

Think about it. If you are a boy or a man reading this, can you even explain how you feel right now? Most of us cannot. Those who could explain it would probably find it a little difficult, unless they are upset, happy, or having some other powerful emotion.

Honestly, many women also struggle to express their specific feelings. Most people will never openly say, "I am hurting," or "I am angry." We usually describe our feelings instead of saying what they are. We will tell you why we are sad without ever telling you that we are sad. Along with that, both women and men are very picky regarding with whom they share their feelings. However, men have a few unique challenges to face when trying to talk about emotions. We may know how we feel . . . but talking about it is completely different.

Men have a different way of communicating.

We will talk about sports, movies, television shows, food, music, video games, comic books, women, or anything else we think may be interesting.

We will not talk about our feelings, emotions, or anything that will lead to immediate drama:

Yes, I know that not sharing my feelings is unhealthy.

No, I still will not talk about it.

Why do I not want to talk about it?

Because it's not going to change anything or make anything better.

No, I will not try anyway.

Why won't I try?

Look, just leave me alone. I don't want to talk about it.

There are some men who are very good at expressing their feelings; however, that is normally not the case. Many men stall and cannot form the right words to explain their feelings. Trying to describe how we feel is like trying to find a drop of water that has fallen into an ocean. It's all mixed up with no way to separate it. Many of us really do not know where to start or where to finish, and we may not even know what we are looking for. We may absolutely *know* what we are feeling; we just may not know *how* to tell you. Many of us can't express it correctly, and every time we try, it's upsetting because we know it is not coming out right.

It is already a challenge to identify our true feelings and find a way to deal with them; now we are expected to open our mouths and speak about something without knowing how.

This may always be a struggle. But when I say that we can't talk about it, it does not mean that it is impossible. "Can't" does not mean that we never will. "Can't" does not mean "won't." "Can't" means that we cannot do it right now. This is good news because one day we will have to talk about how we feel if we plan on becoming successful men.

There are a few things that may make talking about your feelings a little easier (even if it is something that you still don't want to do), and may help with talking in general.

1. THERE ARE GENERALLY TWO WAYS TO TALK ABOUT YOUR FEELINGS:

A. Talk about it until you can figure out what you are feeling ("It's not fair! This is so annoying! If I see him again, I am going to hurt him. I am so mad! He stole my money!")

B. Figure out what you are feeling, then talk about it ("That guy gets me so mad. He always smiles in my face like I don't know that he stole twenty dollars from me!")

Version A seems to be much more common and comes out naturally. Talking about what caused you to feel the way that you do is how many people find out their true emotions. Although this method is common, it can lead to a few problems.

Every boy has had that moment when talking about something emotional causes his words to feel like they're exploding uncontrollably out of his mouth. If you are talking to the right person, this may be a healthy way to figure out your emotions. Sadly, finding someone to listen can be difficult. Boys learn very quickly that there are not many people who want to hear us complain or ramble on about how we feel without judging us. If you find someone who will, take advantage of the opportunity and talk with them.

Another problem with this approach is that along with the explosion of emotion, we may also become aggressive, noisy, and possibly even violent. It's like having a fist full of sand and trying to open your hand just enough to let out one grain—it is as close to impossible as you can get. When we try to talk about our feelings, the same can happen with our emotions. When the emotions that we have struggled so hard to hide have a chance to escape, they take the opportunity. All of a sudden, we may become loud, begin to tear up, or even cry. What started as a calm conversation turns into a challenge to prevent our feelings from taking over.

Version B is simple but can be very hard. You need to know what you are feeling and why you feel that way. That is why many men do not use this version. If we never think about our emotions, how can we talk about them? We won't talk about feelings that we never knew we had. But if you know what you are feeling and can explain why, you may be able to deal with the reason behind your anger (at least what you *think* is anger). Also, if you know what you're feeling and why, you will be able to explain to other people why you are behaving the way you are. That is better than making them guess why you are very quiet, randomly mean, or rude.

Both approaches have their good and challenging points. Although I am sure that there are other great methods, these are the ones that I have seen boys and men successfully use most often.

Pick the one that works best for you, because you should talk and will *have* to talk about how you feel at different times of your life.

2. THINK ABOUT YOUR THOUGHTS

Ask a boy or a man how he feels about something, and you will likely get one of these answers:

"It's OK."

"It was all right."

"Good."

We, as men, tend to use fewer words when talking about emotional topics because this is how we communicate with each other. We know what these answers mean, and we understand the unspoken things that go with them. The details are not necessary for us to understand each other. Explaining details requires talking about emotions, which we already struggle to express.

Many men feel that we are completely logical and rational while girls and women are overly emotional. This is not true. We just try not to express our emotions as often as they do. Our emotions still show up in the kinds of decisions and choices that we make; we still do things because of how we feel. If we were so rational and in control, then we would not struggle to make sense of the hurricane of feelings that we keep locked away.

The brief and general answers that we give, such as "OK" and "all right," make complete sense to us. We don't think that they are short, rude, brief, or disrespectful. We answered the question. We especially don't like giving long answers to things that we think are obvious or things that we simply don't want to talk about. The problem is that these answers are not normally the response that people are looking for. Yet they are the only answers we can come up with. If you are like most of us, it will take you a while before you learn how to better communicate your feelings.

Let's take a look at a commonly frustrating conversation:

GIRLFRIEND: Why do you keep doing that?

BOYFRIEND: Doing what?

GIRLFRIEND: Always answering my questions with short answers.

BOYFRIEND: Those are my real answers.

GIRLFRIEND: You don't have anything else to say? There is no other answer that you can give?

BOYFRIEND: Ask different questions.

That's the solution . . . a different question!

We obviously cannot change what people ask us and how they ask; however, you can translate what you hear.

> A man once told me that whenever someone asks how you feel, what you feel, or about your feelings, translate the question to, "What do you think about it?"

Let's try it out.

I am going to ask you two questions. Pay attention to how your brain comes up with an answer. Try to answer as quickly as possible. Ready?

QUESTION 1: HOW DO YOU FEEL ABOUT TREES?

What was your answer? Did you come up with any specific feelings? If so, how many?

Now, second question.

QUESTION 2: WHAT ARE YOUR THOUGHTS ABOUT TREES?

What was your answer this time? Did you come up with something different from the last answer? Did you notice a difference in how your thoughts formed? Many boys and men see a big difference because "thoughts" are less scary than "feelings." If it helps, that's great. If it does not, that just means this method is not for you.

To recap, when someone asks a question that requires feelings, translate the question and think about your thoughts. Sometimes it may work; sometimes it may not. Either way, I'm sure that you will find this translation method helpful in the different relationships you will have in your life.

3. SAY WHAT YOU MEAN; MEAN WHAT YOU SAY

This point is simple. Whenever you speak, make sure that you are as accurate, consistent, and truthful as possible. Do not take a long time to get to your point or try to avoid answering a question by using a lot of words. Say what you mean.

To be clear, when I say "mean," I am talking about being confident and truthful. Do not be rude or inconsiderate.

Men never want to get caught saying the wrong thing. Men are expected to stand on their word. The second you start to go back and try to change what you said, your point loses credibility. People will stop believing you, your opinion may be ignored, and people will stop trusting you. If you did it, admit it. If you have a true story, stick to it.

This does not mean to argue or get aggressive and disrespectful. It also does not mean that you should say things without thinking about how they will affect others. It simply means to be up front, truthful, concise, and confident when you speak. A good man once told me, "All a man has is his word."

4. USE FEWER WORDS

I had a college professor who kept giving me bad grades on my essays and reports. He always said that I was not being clear. So, I kept trying to do better, and he kept giving me low grades. One day I finally asked what I needed to do to get a better grade. He said, "Everything can be said better with fewer words."

I do not believe that this is always true. Sometimes, things really do need to be explained at length. However, you should try to cut out unnecessary talking.

In our society, men generally do not talk a lot unless they are around friends. If they do, it is often viewed as a bad thing. Try to keep unnecessary and extensive talking to a minimum. Whether this is good, bad, right, or wrong, I don't know. However, that is what's expected of you.

Many men struggle with open communication. We avoid certain conversations, find ourselves speechless, can be too aggressive, or maybe even start talking too much. These few points may help you avoid these and other awkward situations. I hope now, when you don't want to talk about it, it will not be because you can't; it will be because you just do not choose to.

MANHOOD CHALLENGE: Try to learn how to talk about your emotions comfortably. Even if you don't do it often, one day you may need to tell someone how you feel.

Four

Decisions, Decisions, Decisions

THE PRINCIPAL SPOTTED THE boy in the hallway and decided to start the conversation. "Good morning! Are you going to get in trouble today?"

While still digging through his locker, the boy answered, "I don't know."

With a confused look on his face, the man asked, "What do you mean, 'I don't know'? Why don't you know?" It wasn't until after he finished asking the question that he realized he sounded frustrated.

The student shrugged his shoulders. He already knew a lecture was coming, so he chose to just say how he really felt. "Sometimes I get in trouble . . . sometimes I don't."

The man, with his furrowed brow and annoyed expression, stayed quiet while the boy avoided looking at him. The man knew if he said the wrong thing or came across as judgmental, the boy would ignore him the way that he always did. Still, the more he thought about the boy's answer, the angrier it made him.

He was struggling to keep calm. He clenched his teeth and said, "You are acting like life just takes you for a ride. You act like you don't have any say in how your life goes." He was getting more upset the more he talked about it. "Life is not a random roller coaster that you're strapped into that will take you where it wants. Make some choices! Every single day you end up in my office because you don't choose! So right here and now, at the beginning of the day, I'm asking you to choose!"

The boy kept staring into his locker. The man slammed the locker door shut. The boy was stunned, then enraged. "What's wrong with you!" he yelled.

The man stared him in the eye and whispered forcefully, "Decide what kind of day you're going to have, and do what it takes to make that happen. Stop letting life take you for a ride!"

———

You do not end up a man because you get older. There are many boys who think that being a man is just what happens when you live long enough to reach legal age. It is because of this that so many boys don't realize how important it is to take some control over their lives. To be the man you want to be and to reach the goals that you have, you have to make decisions as early as possible that will help you get there.

You cannot and must not trust that life will magically turn you into who you need to be. You cannot trust that it will take you where you want to go. You would not trust that a car without a driver could get you to your destination; you should not trust that life without good choices will turn you into a man.

Making good decisions gives you power over your life that cannot be found anywhere else. No matter what situation you may be in, you will always be able to make a choice. Those choices may be the difference between a successful future and a future that you will regret.

I cannot tell you exactly what decisions to make because your life is your own. Yet there are some things that you should consider as you move ahead in life:

1. EVERY DECISION IS SETTING YOU UP FOR MANHOOD

If I placed an open safe with one billion dollars only ten feet in front of you and told you that you can have the money if you walk to the safe by taking only ten steps, how would you try to get the money? By the way, you can't cheat, jump, run, or use any other clever way to make it easier.

Would you waste steps by not walking in a straight line? Would you still try to cheat even though I already said that you cannot? Or would you walk in a straight line and get the money without risking everything?

The trick to getting the prize is that *there is no trick at all.* If you try anything other than walking straight to the safe, you will not get the prize. Every single step will count. If one step is off or not done correctly, you will not make it. Every step— every decision—is setting you up to get to your goal. If you try to do something other than walk in a straight line during your first few steps and then try to fix it in your last steps, you won't make it.

This same rule applies to everyone's lives. One bad step can possibly mess up your chances of ever reaching your goals. Think about all the things that you want to achieve. Think of the best man that you want to be. The race to get to that goal has already started. It started when you were born.

Some of us were born with a lot of opportunities; some of us were not. Some of us have had people helping us and giving us advice; some of us have not. For some, you already heard this lesson from someone; for others, this may be the first time you have ever heard it. Whoever you are, regardless of whether or not you have opportunities, I'm sure that you have taken some bad steps—we all have.

So, I challenge you to make the best decision possible every time you get the chance. We all need to understand that, although we may have made some mistakes, life is not a ten-foot challenge. We can—you can—still make decisions that can change how the story ends. I challenge you to avoid the arguments, to work as hard as possible, to find and listen to wise advice, and to be the best man that you can be. If you don't learn to do what it takes to make the hard decisions now, you will be an adult still trying to learn a boy's lesson.

2. STOP OVERPAYING!

Imagine walking up to the counter of your favorite fast-food restaurant and ordering a small number of chicken nuggets. The cashier rings up your order and says you owe $150. To your surprise, you look up and see that they have raised the price. The cashier was not joking. This is not a prank. You realize that they really cost $150. Would you still buy those nuggets?

Most of us would not. To everyone I have asked this question to, they say that they would not buy the nuggets. When I ask why not, they tell me that they cost too much. They don't want to pay that much for something that they know is not worth it. Simply put, they don't want to overpay.

The decision not to overpay or to stop overpaying can be used for all decisions we make in our lives. What do you want? How much are you willing to pay for it?

You want to go to bed without studying; but if you do, you will fail your test and have to attend summer school. Is avoiding studying worth that outcome? It is probably not. You would be overpaying.

When we don't make good or smart decisions—or when we don't make any decision at all—we find ourselves overpaying. Think about how many times you have overpaid because you became angry, lost your patience, or were lazy, mean, or even silly. All of those times we overpaid by getting into trouble, losing an opportunity, losing privileges, etc. probably could have been avoided with making better decisions.

I know it's not easy. Still, think about the consequences before you make a decision. Not only that, but be honest about what may happen. Think about the worst thing that may happen, because that may be what you end up paying. Moments of laziness, anger, silliness, and frustration usually cost us much more than we are willing to pay. Next time something doesn't work out the way you wanted it, figure out if there was a different decision you could have made. Figure out if you could have paid less.

3. REPUTATION LEADS TO EXPECTATION

Everyone's reputation follows them. That reputation leads to expectation. For example, if I have a reputation for talking when everyone else is quiet, people will begin to expect me to talk when everyone is quiet. Reputation soon becomes expectation. What boys need to understand is that this happens very quickly in men's lives. If you mess up, you may never get a second chance. If you treat someone poorly, they may never give you a second try to make it up.

I know that may not seem fair, but consider this: Imagine that every time you see me with a red hat, I slap you, and every time I have a blue hat, I don't slap you. So far, I have worn a red hat fifteen times, and you've been slapped fifteen times. One day, I walk in with a blue hat and stroll over to you. I take off the blue hat and slowly pull out a red hat. Are you going to stand there and wait to see if I put on the red hat and slap you, or are you going to do what it takes to avoid getting slapped? I am sure that you would make sure that you don't get hit. But . . . what if I complain, "You are not giving me a chance," that "I didn't even do anything," or "All I did was take out a red hat!" Would my complaining convince you to give me one more try? No, it would not. However, if you *did* give me another chance, it would be because you were trying to be nice.

Many boys don't realize this. They become upset because no one is giving them a chance to fix a problem they started. The punishments hit hard and fast, and many boys are saying, "But I didn't really do anything!" or "They didn't give me a chance to explain!" Every boy should know that:

A. No one has to give you a chance.

B. You may never get a second chance. (If you get one, appreciate it. Don't expect another one.)

C. You should make the best decisions possible every time. You may not have another opportunity to get it right.

Keep a good reputation by making good choices. Life can be very difficult when people expect the worst from you. Remember that no one has to give you chances, so make the best of the chances that you get.

GOOD REPUTATION = GOOD EXPECTATION

* * *

There are a lot of opinions about what is the most important thing about being a successful man. I can honestly admit that I do not know what that thing is. However, I do know that our ability to make good decisions is high on the list. We do not just grow into men; we decide to be men. But we decide to be men while we are still boys. Take your decisions seriously. The ability to make the ones that count is very important to becoming a successful adult and man.

Hurry up and make a decision.

MANHOOD CHALLENGE: But Make every choice using all the information, wisdom, and advice that you can find. Stop overpaying.

Five

Watch Out! There's a Trap!

THE YOUNG MAN SAT on the couch with his fingers repeatedly pressing hard on the video game controller. While talking into his headset, his mother walked in.

"Son," she said.

He tried to act like he did not hear her and kept playing, but his eye twitched when she spoke. He hoped she didn't see it.

"Son, I know you heard me."

"I'm sorry, I didn't hear you," he lied. He took off his

headset.

"We have to talk," she said.

"OK. What's up?"

"You know I'm struggling to keep this apartment and . . ." She paused as she noticed that his eyes kept darting back and forth from the television screen to her face. "Son, please stop playing the game."

"What? I'm listening. I can do both."

She had been here before. She chose to avoid the argument. "Fine," she mumbled. "I need help with the rent. You've been staying here for free since you failed out of college. That was a year and a half ago."

She noticed that he had logged off the game, but she could also see that he wasn't looking at her at all now. "Since school is no longer an option," she continued, "you should be looking for some work. You are twenty-two years old now. You have to do something. You can't just keep staying here for free."

He was just sitting there. He wasn't showing any

emotion on his face, although it was obvious that his breathing had gotten harder and faster. He had become disrespectful the last time that they had this conversation. He said things that he shouldn't have and had even thrown things across the room. In order to keep living there, he'd had to promise to never do that again.

"Son," his mother said, looking for him to respond. He kept his promise; he didn't lose his temper. Without saying anything, he gritted his teeth, stood up, and walked out.

Many boys have seen a young man like this one. It may be a friend, brother, cousin, possibly a father, or maybe a character in a story. There are many reasons why young men may behave this way. I would never claim to know all the specific reasons why a boy or man would show this kind of frustration. But there is one reason for this behavior that *every* man has to deal with at some point in his life. It is because he fell into the trap. There is a hidden trap that is waiting for every boy and man in our culture. What is worse is that if we are caught in it, we may never get out.

Boys and men learn that they are supposed to accomplish things, whatever those things may be. It is our identity—we accomplish, we succeed, we build, and we work. Many times, this creates very successful and driven men. Many men will do whatever it takes to reach their goals. There are men who will protect and provide for their family no matter what the cost may be. There are men who will give anything, take anything, and ultimately do anything for success. Many men are so convinced that they must do these things that they end up overpaying and losing more than they intended. However, there is an even bigger downside. What happens when a man does *not* achieve his goals? What happens when a man cannot do the thing that identifies him as a man? What happens when you cannot do what makes you feel like "you"? Who will you be then, and what will you do?

Many young boys and men become lost, angry, and even depressed. When this happens, many of us give up on putting any real effort into life. Although people don't like the phrase, this can be described as self-pity. You stop trying to succeed because you have been so horribly hurt by the fact that you have failed at something important.

Can you see the trap? Men do what they are supposed to do; they accomplish tasks and reach goals. That is how our society describes men, by action and responsibility, but not much else. Sadly, you will never do everything correctly the first time. You will mess up someday. Now that you didn't do what men are "supposed" to do, what are you? According to many people, you cannot be a man.

Some people want boys and men to just suck it up and get over it. Many of us do just that. But some of us struggle with this depressed feeling and keep falling in the trap. There are also some boys and men who will passionately tell you how much they don't care about their mistakes, and they never try to achieve anything more than average. Some of them are telling the truth. They really don't desire more for their lives. For others, probably for most, they are afraid of messing up and failing. *Failure eats away at a man's identity, and for many men, there is nothing left to work for. This leads to giving up.*

What makes this so hard for many men is that we still want to reach for success, but we cannot force our way out of that depressed feeling. We do not want to be people who have given up on their goals, but we can't seem to change it. We become disappointed in ourselves. Sometimes we are disgusted and frustrated. That may lead to depression. Then finally, we become angry.

This is why many men will get upset when you remind them of their mistakes. Mistakes can slowly eat away at our identity. *We are not weak, we are not overreacting, and we are not immature.* We just have to learn to function and succeed as men, even though we may be fighting one of the hardest battles we have ever fought.

I don't have advice on how to stop it or how society should fix it. What I have are a few things that may help you avoid getting to the point where you give up. Furthermore, just in case you do give up, these things may help you persevere.

PERSEVERE, V., to continue doing something or trying to do something even though it is difficult.

—THE MERRIAM-WEBSTER DICTIONARY

1. TAKE SMALLER BITES

A great friend once told me that life is nothing but a series of projects.

Take smaller bites out of life. If you take the largest bite that you can out of a huge sandwich, you know that there will still be some sandwich left. Would you give up and throw it in the trash because you couldn't eat it all in one bite? No. That would be ridiculous. However, this is what many of us do with life.

Life is so large and so long that we must try to approach it one project at a time. We know that a large sandwich may take a few bites to finish eating. In the same way, you have to complete smaller projects to be successful in life. Look at everything you have to do as its own project. Some projects will work out better than others. Just make sure you try your hardest on the next one.

A lot of the pressure that comes with manhood can be managed and even avoided with good decisions and organization. For the other pressures that are going to come, no matter what you do, work on it one project at a time. If you fail at one, you have the next one. Even if you have messed up to the point that life will never be the same, find the next project and give it everything that you have. Tackle each project with excellence. The faster you conquer the next project, the faster you can let go of your failures.

No matter what, do not fall into that trap of feeling so bad about your failures that you stop trying. Never give up. Again, it is all just a series of projects. Take smaller bites out of life so you will be able to finish strong and be happy with the result. Start small and accomplish the little things. You will find that the little things will start adding up to big things.

2. DON'T EXPECT CREDIT. USE CRITIQUE.

There are some boys and men who give up on trying to accomplish tasks because they are not getting credit for the work that they are doing. All the effort of pushing past anger and pain, all the patience and dedication you have shown, ignoring all the comparisons to other people, and no one wants to give you credit?! Then why keep trying at all?

When you are young, you don't always have a major goal to reach. As a result, you don't have anything to work for other than the recognition and credit that other people give you. When you don't receive that credit, you may wonder, *Why keep working at all?* What can make this worse is that people (especially men) will criticize you, telling you everything that you are doing wrong. This makes many boys and men just want to give up even more.

So how do we handle this? How do we deal with not getting credit for the battles we have won and instead being insulted and criticized for our mistakes?

63

Please allow me to be straightforward and clear. It is very important that you understand what you are about to read: **NO ONE HAS TO GIVE YOU CREDIT FOR ANYTHING.** Would it be nice to be recognized for our accomplishments? Sure. Would it be nice if people (especially men) did not always find something wrong with us? Yes. But as boys and men, we are always being trained to be better. It is similar to practicing for a sport. When practicing, you don't celebrate every time you do things correctly. You try to fix everything that is wrong. In life, everyone is your coach. People are constantly trying to get you to reach a level of manhood and success that you have never reached. You will not get credit as much as you would like. You will be criticized more than you want. Use that to your advantage.

Find a personal goal and focus on it. This way, even if no one gives you credit for what you have done, you still have a goal to reach. Focus on finishing the projects you need to in order to reach your goal. When it comes to critique, use it! Everybody doesn't have good advice, but it's not that hard to figure out what's good and what's not. When you are young, listen to as much good advice as you can. Find people you trust who are wise and smart. Listen to what they have to say. You cannot use all advice, but you can listen to it. It can only make you better.

3. KNOW THAT YOU ARE MORE THAN WHAT YOU DO

Yes, men are known by what they do, what they accomplish, and what they achieve, but this should not be the only way that we identify ourselves. If it is, then we are setting ourselves up to be caught in the trap. Even if other people only identify us by what we do, we have to be aware that we are more than that.

Boys and men have to know that they must have character. Yes, character. Your character is your behavior, traits, and qualities that make up who you are. We use words like "morals," "ethics," "honor," and "integrity" when we talk about a person's character. How do you affect the people around you? What do people think of you? Would you help people who are in need or let them suffer? Do you want to make the world a better place, or do you not think about it? As a man, do you want to be a good father, maybe an example for young boys, or do you not care?

If you have character, then you can identify yourself as more than what you do. So just in case you do mess up every now and then, you will still have an identity and a fight in you to push through disappointment. We all can be disappointed and even depressed, but who you are—your character—gives you what you need in order to push through. You are so much more than what you do, because what you do all depends on who you are.

Again, I know that these are not the only reasons that boys and men get trapped in disappointment. I also know that there are other things that can motivate us. However, understanding this trap, how to avoid it, and how to fight it is a useful piece of information to help us be successful men. Bite off pieces of life at a time; complete each project. Remember that you don't need credit, but you can always use criticism to your advantage.

Finally, remember that you need character; who you are will control what you do.

MANHOOD CHALLENGE: Do what you need to do despite how you may feel.

Six

Every Man Isn't a Man

HIS SISTER FINALLY CAME through for him.

After months and months of her refusing to do so, she got him courtside tickets and special access. She said it was his early birthday present. He always figured that she didn't want her little brother messing up her image, but this time she was being the cool older sister he remembered. He missed that time when it was the two of them against the world.

The boy was starstruck.

He could not believe that he was actually in the locker room meeting the players of his favorite team. He was amazed at the size and details of the locker room. It looked like an office, a locker room, a living room, and a sports bar all in one. But that was not what really excited him. He was waiting for one important person—his sister's new boyfriend, his favorite player. His mom loved that his sister was dating someone rich. His dad wasn't around enough to know what was going on. And when their dad did come around, he brought his issues with him.

He was in the backseat of a limousine!

As a fan, he was having a great time. After visiting the locker room, his sister and the season MVP decided to go out to eat. He had a signed jersey, a hat, pictures, and, most of all, memories. The music in the stretch SUV was loud enough to enjoy but low enough to still have a conversation. His sister and her boyfriend, the superstar nicknamed Dr. Strange, were cuddled up across from him.

Strange was the boy's idol. They'd had a similar home life, they went to the same kind of school, and they grew up in the same kind of neighborhood. There was no one else the boy had ever seen as a role model.

Strange's gigantic bodyguard, Less, sat looking out of the window. The bodyguard didn't seem happy about working tonight. The boy wondered what was on his mind.

The restaurant's private room was filled with other athletes, music stars, and even one or two billionaires . . . and their bodyguards. He was going to remember this as the best night ever.

When it was time to leave, Strange patted him on the head and told the boy to head to the limousine while he paid for the meal. The boy made his way out, leaving a room of the richest people he'd ever met. While walking out of the restaurant, his heart skipped a beat and he froze. Did he hear that? Then he heard it again. He turned around and tried to run back into the restaurant, but one of the other bodyguards wouldn't let him in.

"That's my sister screaming!" he yelled at the bodyguard. He knew the sound of his sister screaming in pain. He heard it every time his father drank too much. He had heard it too many times.

"Sorry, little man," the guard said. "Can't let you in. Everything is good, though. They will be out in a minute."

There was shouting and ruckus coming from the back of the restaurant. The boy was fighting to get past the guard when he finally caught a glimpse of what was going on in the restaurant. He saw Strange grabbing his sister by the arms and shaking her violently.

Then he saw the first hit to her face; then the second. The boy glanced around at all the rich people who looked uncomfortable but weren't doing anything to stop it.

"Stop him!" the boy shouted at the top of his lungs.

Three hits.

Four.

"Stop!"

Five.

"Stop it!"

Six.

"Stop!"

Less, the bodyguard, came and grabbed Strange before he could throw another strike. Strange looked at him angrily but then calmed down. He threw his crying girlfriend to the side, fixed his clothes, and went to grab his coat from the private room.

After getting his things, he turned to leave the restaurant. Walking to the door, he looked at the crying girl and said, "Fix your face and let's go." Crying and bruised, she stood up and got in line behind Strange.

The boy just stood still outside of the doorway. He was

frozen in shock. Why is she doing what he says? He just beat her!

Less walked out in front of the couple with a look of disgust on his face. He put his hand on the boy's shoulder. "Come on, man," he said. The boy turned around to go back to the limousine but kept his eyes on his sister behind him.

"Turn around," she said. She was ashamed. He could see it in her eyes. He had seen it before.

They were in front of their house now. During the entire ride he stared and glowered at Strange, but Strange was too busy talking on the phone to notice. His sister sat quietly sniffling every now and then.

Strange did not bother with getting out of the car.

Less opened the car door for the siblings, and the three of them walked up to the house. "Thanks, Less," she croaked, and went inside.

"Thanks, Less," the boy mumbled. He moved to go inside when he felt Less's hand on his shoulder.

"Hey," Less said softly. The boy turned around to look at the huge wall of a man. Less leaned in with concern and said, "I'm going to say something that you always need to remember. Are you listening?"

The boy nodded. "I know you looked up to Strange. And he's a great athlete, without a doubt," Less said. "But when you are picking men like him for your role models, when you are trying to figure out what kind of man you want to be, be very careful." Less leaned down and looked the boy in the eye. "Because every man isn't a man."

Less waited. Then he followed up, "You understand?"

Again, the boy nodded.

"Less, let's go," Strange yelled from the limo. "These girls just texted me that they want to come over!"

Less looked at the boy and made a face that said, See what I mean?

WARNING!

DO NOT FOLLOW THE EXAMPLE OF EVERY MAN!

Any male of legal age is considered a man, but that does not mean that he understands manhood. He may use the title of "man," but that does not mean that he understands what that means. Every person who is called a man is not a man. Be very careful about who you make your role models. Don't try to become like any and every example that you see. Following a bad example can make growing into a successful man harder than it is already.

There are many men who have become successful athletes, musicians, and businessmen. Some have had a lot of relationships, are very popular, and seem like they have everything a boy could dream of. Do not confuse this with being a man. Honestly, some of these men may be trying to make themselves feel better about not being a *complete* man.

If a man is good in business or very successful in some

part of his life, that does not make him a successful man. It makes him successful in that specific field. If you want him as a role model, use him as an example of how to succeed in that field. Yet never forget, that does not automatically mean that he is a good man.

One reason I am writing this book is because I have seen too many boys, young men, and even adult men try to live their entire lives like their role models. The problem is, in my opinion, their role models do not always live the kind of lives that men should live. Sometimes we find out that these people have done things that they shouldn't do: hurt, kill, steal, lie, cheat, and much more. Sadly, there are boys and men who end up saying that they want to be just like them. Many boys even make excuses for their role models when they do something wrong; or even worse, many boys don't think that these things are wrong at all.

Remember, just because you are good at something, just because you can succeed in a certain field, does not mean that you are a successful man. If being a successful man is what you are aiming to be, then these questions should always have a

positive answer:

HOW DO YOU AFFECT THE PEOPLE AROUND YOU?

WHAT DO PEOPLE THINK OF YOU?

WOULD YOU HELP SOMEONE IN NEED OR LET THEM
SUFFER?

DO YOU WANT TO MAKE THE WORLD A BETTER PLACE,
OR DO YOU NOT THINK ABOUT IT?

DO YOU WANT TO BE A GOOD EXAMPLE FOR YOUNG
BOYS, OR DO YOU NOT CARE?

IS MAKING A LOT OF MONEY IN THE FUTURE YOUR
ONLY GOAL?

DO YOU CARE WHO MIGHT GET HURT WHILE YOU ARE
BECOMING FINANCIALLY SUCCESSFUL?

ARE YOUR FEELINGS AND GETTING WHAT YOU WANT
ALL THAT REALLY MATTER?

DO YOU EVER THINK ABOUT WHAT KIND OF FATHER,
HUSBAND, OR LEADER YOU WOULD BE?

HOW DO YOU WANT PEOPLE TO REMEMBER YOU WHEN

YOU DIE?

A man should care about more than money, his job, fame, and fortune. A man who is selfish is only good to himself and harmful to everyone else. Furthermore, a man should always be thinking about his family, if he has one, and his community. Even as a boy, you should be working on being a man who will build his family, be a dependable and loyal husband, and be a great example of a man for his children. What a man wants should not be the only thing that matters; it should not even be the most important thing. The world needs unselfish men to help, provide, and change what is wrong.

Every man does not do this, but many men will agree that all men should. Every man has areas that he still needs to work on. The problem is, we usually don't see many of them working on anything but fame and fortune.

Many adults have never had an example of a man in their lives. They never had a man show them how they should live their lives. They had to figure it out for themselves. Many of these men are just doing what they feel is best; however, that does not mean that it is right. Remember, even though some men are older, they are still working out their boy issues.

Some of these men have done very well in their careers. They have done things in their lives that we can look up to and even follow. But we should be careful and make sure that we do not follow bad examples of manhood. Remember, men are more than what they do. Professional success does not equal manhood. Find an example of a man who is more than what he has done. Follow a man's example because he has character. Follow a man because of who he is and not because of what he has done. A man with professional success may not always be successful, but a man with character will always be a man.

MANHOOD CHALLENGE: When looking at role models, remember that each man is made up of different parts. Which parts do you want? Which parts should you avoid?

SEVEN

MAN UP AND GET HELP

HE COULDN'T SLEEP AGAIN. He was tossing and turning in bed when he noticed a faint light reflecting down the hallway. He slowly sat up in the bed and placed his feet on the floor without causing the hardwood to creak. Carefully, he tiptoed over to his bedroom closet, cracked the door open, and reached into his brother's golf bag. Now armed with a golf club, he made his way toward the light, ready to attack whoever was in his house. A few footsteps later, he put the club down.

His son was sitting at the kitchen table drinking soda.

It was 2 A.M.

"Son? You all right? It's very late," he said.

"I'm OK, Dad," the boy responded. "Just thinking."

"About what?"

The boy shrugged. "Life, I guess."

The father looked at the clock and thought about how early he had to wake up for work in the morning. That didn't matter.

The father went to the counter and poured himself a glass of water. He glanced over at his son and then walked over to the cabinet to grab a bag of potato chips. He carried the chips and the water over to the table and took a seat next to his son. "What's going on?"

His son didn't move for a few seconds. The only noise in the house was the sound of crunching as his father ate the sour cream and onion flavored chips.

"You hate sour cream and onion," the son said quietly.

"Yeah . . . but they were your uncle's favorite," the father responded. "Helps me deal with it, I guess."

There was silence again.

"Help me with these, would ya," the dad asked. "I'm fat enough as it is."

The son grabbed a few and began to snack as he drank his soda.

His father continued, "What's up? Talk to me."

"I don't know," his son whispered. "Just trying to figure some stuff out."

"Like what?"

"I don't know." He placed his forehead in his hand and continued, "I mean . . . I'm seventeen years old. I don't know what school I want to go to. I don't know what I want to do with my life. Gina wants to go to school across the country, and I don't know what that's going to mean for our relationship. Up until last month, I thought that I would get an athletic scholarship, but ever since I hurt my shoulder schools have stopped talking to me . . ."

"Yeah," his dad said as he just kept eating and listening.

"I keep having dreams about Uncle Kevin."

"Yeah, me too."

"I still can't believe he's gone."

His dad stayed silent and took a sip of water.

"How do you deal with it?" the son asked.

"Well . . ." the father began. "Son, you just have to accept that sometimes people die."

"Yeah. But that's different from accepting suicide. How do you handle that?"

His dad stayed quiet for a few seconds as he stared at the tablecloth.

"Honestly?" he asked.

His son looked at him, waiting for him to continue.

The father smirked and said, "I found a support group

of men who have lost loved ones to suicide. They help me through a lot. And your mom has been a great shoulder to lean on."

The son's face gave away his surprise. His dad was the hardest and toughest man he had known: veteran, construction worker, former Golden Gloves boxing champ, former amateur MMA fighter . . . the list went on. Picturing him sitting in a circle talking about his feelings was . . . weird.

"I can't see you doing that. Maybe the mom thing, but not the group."

His dad chuckled. "Why not?"

"Just didn't see you as the kind of guy to look for that kind of help."

He took another sip of water. "Yeah, well, it took a while for me to get to that point, but you have to get help when you need it."

"Is that where you got this eating his favorite potato chips thing from?"

"Yeah, they said to hold on to some things that represented him."

The boy laughed. "That's why you took up golf!"

His dad smiled and nodded.

"Let that go, Dad. You're horrible," his son playfully pleaded.

The dad was in the middle of drinking his water when he laughed and water began to go up his nose. His son openly let out a belting laugh at the sight of his father almost choking on his drink.

The father continued laughing as he used his hand to catch the water that was running down his face. "I'm not that bad. I'm all right," he said laughing.

"All wrong," his son quipped.

The father finished chuckling and composed himself.

"Listen, you have a lot of decisions to make and a lot of thinking to do. Don't do it all by yourself."

"I know," the son said. "And I'm trying to be a man about it but—"

"What does that mean?" the father asked.

His son, surprised, asked, "What does what mean?"

"Trying to be a man about it," the father responded with curiosity.

"Like, I'm trying to do it myself and stay strong. I mean, I'm not trying to burden other people with my issues."

The father looked at his son while he finished chewing a chip. He grabbed a napkin, started wiping off his hands, and then leaned in.

"Son, I know that the music you listen to, the movies you watch, and all the encouraging stories about men always tell the story of some man who is 'self-made' or made it without anyone helping him."

The father leaned in even closer. "No one makes it on their own. Someone helped. Someone hired you, someone picked you or referred you, someone bought something for you, someone gave you advice, and someone gave you a chance to prove yourself.

"Don't let that myth about the self-made man have you stressed out and driving yourself crazy. Being a man is way too hard to do it by yourself. If you really want to be a man, man up and get help."

————

One of the biggest problems of becoming a man is that we are taught not to ask for help. Boys are encouraged to figure things out and fix problems by themselves. Being able to do this is something that you can brag about as a man. "I fixed it," "I solved it," "I worked it out," "No one helped me," "I did it"—these are all things that we can be proud of (and we should be proud). However, "I don't need any help" and "I got it" are good ways to make life very hard. Being a man means that you have to learn how to do things on your own, but you will still need help.

I decided to write *8 Things Every Boy Should Know about Being a Man* because I noticed that there are boys who could use some extra help on their journeys to becoming great men. Trying to figure out how to live a man's life on your own without having a real example to follow is something that no boy should have to do, yet so many have no other choice. We all need help, and every man learns this at some point in his life. There are very few things that you can do in life without someone's help. Someone has to hire you for a job. Someone has to accept you into a school. Someone has to give you a chance. You cannot even have a conversation without someone listening and responding. If you want to go somewhere that you've never been, someone or something has to give you directions. There are too many boys who don't have anyone or anything to give them directions on their way to manhood. What's even worse is that there are even more men who do not *want* directions.

So many people know that men don't like to take directions. I mean, there are jokes, television commercials, comedies, and even movie scenes about it. Let's explore what would happen if men *did* ask for directions. What would happen if they asked for help?

If mature men asked for help from the right people, they could solve problems faster, learn lessons easier, and waste less time in life. If that is what men could do, imagine what boys could do if they received the same help. Imagine how many mistakes they would never make. Imagine how many lessons they would learn. Imagine how much easier it would be to succeed.

I know that some of you will think, *So, who do I ask?* Maybe you will wonder, *Who can I trust to help me?* If you know a man who fits the description of a "good man" in this book, ask him. You can also trust certain women to help you as well. Find someone who is smart and who cares. If you can, find someone with life experience. But don't try to figure life out all on your own unless that is your only choice.

> You can always learn something from any and every man—what to do, or what not to do.

We all have had some man influence us. At some point in life there was a man who was close to us, or maybe even a man who we did not personally know, who gave us advice or an example to follow. He could have been a coach, a teacher, a family member, a mentor, a celebrity, a politician, a clergyman, or even a historical figure. But that little leadership helps us. Sadly, for some of us who had the wrong example, it did more damage than good in our lives. (Remember, you should be looking for an example of a *complete* man.) The point is that a man knows when he needs to get help. That is how he grows and develops into a better man. Boys and young men need to learn this same lesson.

Many men who abuse drugs, drink alcohol until they cannot function, mistreat women, and perform other destructive acts do it because they are struggling with something and do not have help. It may be because they cannot identify what they are feeling; it may be because they cannot talk about their problems; it may be because they have fallen into the trap, or any number of reasons; yet, if they had some help, maybe things would be better.

"Man up" and get help. People don't have to be kind or help you, so take advantage of it when you can. I don't know where I would be if I didn't have the example, advice, and leadership of men who had already learned life lessons. However, if you have to do it alone, don't feel too bad. Learn from the lives of great men in history; read books, watch documentaries, learn and use their lives as examples. There are many great men who had to teach themselves. If you know you need help, get some. "Man up" and know your limitations. "Man up" and get help.

MANHOOD CHALLENGE: Ask for help before things get too hard.

Eight

What I Never Said

EVERYTHING WAS TAKEN FROM him.

He did not even have his clothes anymore.

He had been strip-searched . . . thoroughly.

He had been given a uniform.

He had been given a cellmate.

His cellmate did not look happy.

The cell also had an open toilet.

It always smelled.

He had been there six months.

He was a tad more muscular, although you wouldn't be able to tell while he was wearing a shirt. He was noticeably more scarred and bruised. He was noticeably angrier. He was also noticeably happy to have a visitor—his father.

"How are you holding up in here?" his father asked.

"Eh. Same as always," the prisoner replied.

"Yeah," the dad said with a sigh.

The father sniffed as he stared his boy in the eye. His last visit was the first time that he had not cried while talking to his son. One visit without crying—a new record. With this visit he was aiming for two. Although it still hurt to visit his son in prison, he was no longer shocked to see him as a prisoner; he was just disappointed.

"Mom sends her love as always," he said to his son.

The son smiled. "Thanks. How is she doing?"

"Doing well. All she does nowadays is volunteer at that after-school program."

"Wow, that's new. Good for her. How long has she been doing that?"

The father looked over his son's shoulder at the room behind him. He looked to his right at the correction officer who was standing as a sentinel. He knew that the answer would hurt his son's feelings and he didn't want to do that. Nevertheless, he chose to be honest. He rubbed his head nervously and said,

"She's been volunteering since you were sentenced."

"Oh," the son said shamefully. "Think she's trying to stay busy?"

"Actually, no. I think she's . . . I think . . . honestly, I'm sure that she looks at the kids in the program as if they were you. She thinks she did something wrong with you, so she's trying to do something right with them."

"She didn't do anything wrong," the son said with a cracking voice and glossy eyes. "Nothing wrong at all. Please tell her I said that."

His father just stared at his hand, which was resting on the table in front of him. His son's comments made him think about a question that he had been wondering about ever since the trial. Well, more specifically, he had been thinking about it ever since he saw his son crying after hearing his sentence. He finally thought that it was the right time to ask.

"Since you mentioned that, if you don't mind me asking, uh . . . what happened?"

His son looked confused.

The dad clarified, "How did things get to the point that you had to hit her?"

The father had never seen his son look so disgusted before. He looked away from his father, slightly rolling his eyes.

"You know how it goes, Dad," the son began. "Women are so emotional that it's ridiculous."

The father adjusted himself in his seat and motioned for his son to continue.

His son leaned in. "I came in late one night from hanging out with my friends, and she started questioning me like I was a criminal or something."

The father noticed that his son started to get upset as he went on with his story.

"She kept talking and talking. I told her I was going to go get some air. On my way out the door she stood in front of me and told me I needed to 'be a man.' One thing led to another. Now I'm here."

The father became very curious. "Why would she say that?" he asked. "Was she just upset, or had you two been having problems?"

His son shrugged and said dispassionately, "She was annoyed that I stopped trying to go back to school. She said that I was unreliable. And she was always talking about the fact that I wasn't living up to my potential. She wanted me to go see a counselor or psychologist." He chuckled. "That wasn't going to happen."

"I didn't know that you stopped going to school."

"I just didn't feel that it was for me."

The dad's face changed from curiosity to concern, but he let his son continue.

"Anyway, she had all these complaints, and any time we were together she was always being overly emotional and irrational. But that's how women are . . ."

"I never taught you that," the father whispered while shaking his head in disapproval. "Who taught you that?"

"What? What are you talking about?"

"Who taught you to look at women that way? I didn't."

"What are you talking about? It's common knowledge."

The dad was trying to control his frustration. "Let me ask you something. If you thought that she was as clear-headed as you, if you thought that she was as good at controlling her emotions as you—keep in mind that you beat her up—do you think things would have gotten so bad that you would have beat up your future wife?"

"What?"

"Here is what I am asking: if you respected her feelings and reactions, do you think that you would have reacted the way that you did?"

The son sat in seething silence. He was angry. Very angry. The father noticed that the officer was looking at the two of them with much more interest. He must have picked up on their rising voices and tense body language. The dad decided to try and calm down.

"Sorry," he said honestly. "You have enough to deal with without me ticking you off. I asked and you answered. Thank you." However, his son was still upset.

"You act like being a man is easy," the son said with bitterness in his voice. "Like a real man will never make mistakes and should be perfect."

"No," the father whispered confusedly while shaking his head. "I have never said that."

"You always wanted me to be some perfect man that you created."

"Not at all, son. I have never said any of that."

"You always wanted me to be soft and overly caring. It's like you wanted me to be a girl. You don't know how to raise a man."

"Who do you think you're talking to?" the father sneered, trying to keep his voice down.

"Do you know why I'm here?" the son asked angrily.

"I'm here because I'm a man who was not going to allow someone to disrespect me."

The officer swiftly began walking over.

The son didn't notice.

"I made my own choices!"

The officer called for backup.

The father, getting nervous, whispered, "Son, calm down."

The son was too furious to listen.

"And I was not about to let my woman question my manhood!"

The father was shocked, stunned, and confused. When he could not hold it any longer, he began to yell, "What are you talking about? Who taught you this stuff?"

Sadly, there would be no answer. The officers grabbed the prisoner—his son—by the arms. The son violently snatched one of his arms away.

"Get your hands off me," he barked.

He should have seen it coming. It felt like a football player tackled him from behind.

He was facedown on the floor with two officers on his back. Even if he'd wanted to move, he couldn't.

He heard his father yelling to the officers, "Stop! Stop! That's not necessary!"

They pulled the prisoner up to his feet and began to

walk him out of the door. He never looked back at his father. If he had, he would have seen his father crying. There went the record.

Another officer came in to get the father and lead him out. He was still thinking about his son. He never noticed the guard.

"Sir," the officer said to get his attention, "it's time to go."

The father just looked in his direction and nodded. He followed the officer and whispered through his sniffles, "I never said that."

In this last chapter, I want to focus on the things that I have not mentioned. The things that I never said are very important. I have already written that I never said being a man is easy. I also never said that figuring out your emotions or communicating your feelings were easy. Honestly, most men would probably agree that no part of manhood is simple, easy, or light. Yet there are more unspoken things that every boy should know.

Here are eight things I *never* said:

I NEVER SAID THAT DOING THESE THINGS IS PAINLESS.

There are suggestions I have given in this book that will be very uncomfortable. We as men all struggle with some of these things; however, conquering them can help us in our lives. Don't let the uncomfortable feelings stop you from becoming a better man.

I NEVER SAID THAT EVERY MAN DOES ALL EIGHT THINGS.

We are all trying to be the best men that we know how to be. That does not mean that we always get things right. It also does not mean that we all do the things in this book. Some men have never learned these lessons; some men are still working on them; some do not agree with all of them. Don't judge a man too harshly. He may still be trying to figure things out. However, you don't have to wait until manhood; you have the ability to learn these lessons now.

I NEVER SAID THAT ALL EIGHT THINGS WILL APPLY TO YOUR LIFE RIGHT NOW.

Depending on how old you are and what you have experienced in your life, some of the lessons may not matter to you right now. That is OK. I am certain that they all will make sense at some time. Life has a way of surprising you. These eight things are just trying to make sure that you are prepared.

I NEVER SAID THAT THESE EIGHT THINGS ARE ALL YOU NEED TO KNOW ABOUT BEING A MAN.

There are many more lessons you will need to learn as you get older. These eight are just basic steps to help you develop. Think about it like a house—you cannot build a second floor until you have built the first. These eight things are meant to help you build the first floor of manhood. The other lessons that you learn will be adding on more floors.

I do not have all the answers. I know that there is much more for me to learn. Nevertheless, I have listened to the great men who are in my life and those who came before me. The lessons in this book are a result of their wisdom combined with my life experiences. Because I am still living, I still have more to experience. With every new experience, I will learn more.

* * *

There is one area I must address—girls and women. I have not mentioned a lot about them because I am focusing on boys' and men's issues. Here's what I never said about girls and women:

I NEVER SAID THAT GIRLS AND WOMEN ARE IRRATIONAL.

IRRATIONAL, ADJ., not thinking clearly: not able to use reason or good judgment.

—THE MERRIAM-WEBSTER DICTIONARY

"Irrational" simply means that someone's thoughts do not make sense.

Many men believe that women never think clearly. This is not true. Women and men, boys and girls do not always see things the same way. But to say that girls and women are irrational means that we as boys and men always feel as if we think the right way. Again, this is not true. There is not always a right way of thinking. Many times, there are just different ways of thinking.

Men can be irrational, but no one really says anything. A woman or a girl may do something that we don't understand and we call her "crazy." But if girls and women were so irrational, they would not perform better than boys in school. If many of us were to be honest, the smartest person you know is probably a girl or a woman.

The next time a girl or a woman does something that you don't understand, remember that she may just see things differently than you do.

I NEVER SAID THAT GIRLS AND WOMEN ARE OVERLY EMOTIONAL.

The real issue is that men are so used to not showing or seeing emotion that when we see it, we become uncomfortable. A girl suddenly crying or yelling is ultimately the same thing as a boy hitting someone because he became angry. They are both outbursts of emotions; however, when men do it, people don't judge them. A woman deciding that she doesn't want to talk because she is upset is the same show of emotion as a man who doesn't want to talk because he doesn't want to have an outburst of anger. Again, when we do it, we are trying to control emotions; when they do it, they are being emotional. We spend so much time trying not to show our emotions that we think girls and women show theirs too much. We may be different, but we're not better.

I NEVER SAID THAT GIRLS AND WOMEN ARE NOT EQUAL TO BOYS AND MEN.

We live in a world where girls and women are not treated equally to boys and men. They have to fight harder, prove themselves more than men, and are not always allowed to do the same things as men.

This is not right.

This is not fair.

As boys and men, we should be trying our hardest to make sure that we treat women like the equals that they are.

Although this book is talking about boys' and men's issues, we should never forget that women struggle with an entirely different set of problems. Many of these problems we cannot and will not completely understand because we are not women. It's the same way that women cannot completely understand our issues as men. We should work to understand and respect women, their issues, and their struggles. We should work to change the unfair ways that they are treated.

I NEVER SAID THAT WE SHOULD DISRESPECT WOMEN.

Due to the fact that girls and women are not seen as equal to men, men get away with disrespecting them. Girls and women should not be seen as objects for men to use or to be talked about as if they were lesser people. We do not own them. They are not ours to use. Women are not ours to punish or correct. They are as smart as we are, if not smarter. They can do the same work that we can do, if not better. We should not disrespect them by treating them as if they are here to work for and entertain us. If you think that you are an honest, honorable, trustworthy, loyal, and dependable boy or man, the girls and women in your life should see you behave that way.

Every man who reads this book will be able to come up with many more positive things that I never said. If you are that man, I challenge you to pass those things along to a boy. If you are a boy, find a wise and positive man who shows you a real-life example of what is in this book, and teaches you the things that are not.

Becoming a man is like walking on a long road with no map to get to a place that you have never been. You can only follow the advice of the men who have walked the road before you, and try to make the best decisions when you come to a place that no one has told you about. Don't give up or get so tired that you stop learning. I never said that it would be easy, but I did say that it is doable. It is manageable, and it is winnable.

MANHOOD CHALLENGE: Keep working to become a complete man. Remember that some lessons take a little longer to learn. Never forget to treat women the way you want to be treated.

Conclusion: Three Wishes

THERE ARE MANY MORE things that every boy should know about being a man. These eight are just a few things that will help build a foundation. If you do not have an active man in your life who is a good example, the lessons in this book can help you begin to understand some of the complicated things about manhood. Although life can give you good times and bad times, hold on to these lessons. They will help you become a man who can thrive in those moments.

I have always believed that if you can do something about a problem, don't wish or hope. Do something. This handbook is my effort to better young boys' and men's lives. Now that the book is complete, I have a few hopes and wishes.

My first wish is that this book will make moving from

a boy to a man a little easier. Is it difficult? Yes, but becoming a good man is worth it. A good man can achieve his personal goals while also being support for his family, an amazing husband, a magnificent father to his children, and an example of manhood for boys—and, quite simply, change the world in his own way. The world needs more men like that.

My second wish is that you become that kind of man—a man who knows his feelings and controls his anger, and a man who can communicate and solve problems. That man can avoid unnecessary violence and self-destructive behavior. That man's ability to work out and communicate his feelings and thoughts will allow him to make good decisions for his life and for the lives that depend on him. He will not give up because life becomes difficult; he will persevere. It is like changing a period at the end of a sentence into a comma. A period means that the sentence or the thought is finished. A comma means that there is just a quick pause, a brief break. A man's ability to never give up will turn the periods in his life to commas. Giving up when life gets difficult means that you are stopping at that part of your life and nothing good will happen afterward. Perseverance transforms those stops into pauses. In other words, perseverance—not giving up—can take a moment that looks like nothing will happen and make something happen. What could have been a period in your life will become a comma.

My final wish is that as you become a complete man, you will influence other boys to want to be complete as well. When you become that man, you can give boys a different image of manhood than what they may normally see. They will be inspired to be a man who is actually a man. Boys will look at you and be able to tell the difference between a man who is only good at his job and a man who is good at being a man. In you they will see a man who gets help when he needs it, never needing to resort to suicide or drug and alcohol addiction. They will also see a man who does not look down on other men but provides help if he can. They will see in you a man who respects women and holds them in the highest regard.

I hope that this book helps you become that man. No matter where you are in life, no matter what example you have or do not have, no matter what mistakes you have made or will make, you can still be the great man that you are destined to be.

* * *

If you are reading this book, then this is just your halftime. Whatever you have or have not done so far is your halftime score, and the halftime score is useless, because the game isn't over. There is still time to do what you need to do.

Becoming a man is a lifelong process. Start wherever you can and do the best that you can do. Some things will come easier than others, but continue to work and learn as much as you can. All men have had to struggle at some point with manhood. The goal is to persevere and push through. Remember, one day there will be another boy who will be waiting to learn from a man like you.

Thank you for reading *8 Things Every Boy Should Know About Being A Man*. I hope it was useful. If you would like to help bring more attention to this book, please leave a review on the book platform of your choice. A few minutes and a few words will go a long way.

If you would like to receive free tools and resources, or just sign up for my email list for updates, please visit:

www.horacchoughauthor.com

Acknowledgments

To every boy I have been lucky enough to work with, thank you. *8 Things* are the lessons that we have learned together. To the most amazing Kellee Hough, this book would not exist without your invaluable and indelible support. Patrick Price, thank you for enheartening me to own my voice. Moreover— see what I did there—I could not have asked for a better and more professional editor. Dave Valenica and Christina Roth, thank you for your scalpels. To the boys of Pathways Academy and Messiah, before I ever put words in a document, working with you showed me how much I care about your futures. Alex and Kevin, although you were my mentees, you mentored me more than you will ever know. Brandon, Jonathan, Daquan, Sebastian—in no particular order—from being boys I worked with to becoming men who are my friends, you changed my life and taught me many things about myself.

Destin, my first beta reader, not only were you my target audience, you were my most important critic. Thank you for your thoughts and insight. Solomon and Jake, you confirmed that I was on the right track and gave me confidence to continue writing this handbook. Anita Rice, you are amazing. I challenge anyone to find a comb with a finer tooth. Mary Ronan, this project was written with my words through your modeling and encouragement. To the men in my life who are thoroughly immersed in the spirit of friendship, thank you for lifting as you climb. R. Ford, you are That Man. Thank you for pushing me to make this happen. Hough and Lanier men, thank you for showing me how to do it right. Finally, to the most invaluable resources and teachers, Walter and Bonnie Hough, thank you for raising me to be a man who understands the need to help others.

ABOUT THE AUTHOR

HORACE HOUGH HAS WORKED with urban and suburban youth through mentoring, education, and nonprofit organizations for twenty years. His time as an administrator at an all-boys middle school, working as director of an all-boys mentoring program, and decades of community work with young men have inspired him to provide as many tools as possible for boys to navigate adulthood. Horace was born and raised in New York and currently resides in Connecticut.

Made in United States
Orlando, FL
28 January 2022

14180365R00083